HOW TO
DOODLE
EVERYWHERE

CUTE & EASY DRAWINGS
FOR NOTEBOOKS, CARDS,
GIFTS AND SO MUCH MORE!

KAMO

TUTTLE Publishing

Tokyo | Rutland, Vermont | Singapore

Contents

Let's Doodle!

Hey, everyone, I'm Kamo, and while I'm an illustrator by trade, I'm also a mad doodler.

My approach to drawing is simple: If you know the basics, you can draw anything. Take a lion, for example. Make a circle, add the ears, face and mane and—voila!—you're done. It really is that easy to get started. Before you know it, you'll be doodling everywhere with a style all your own.

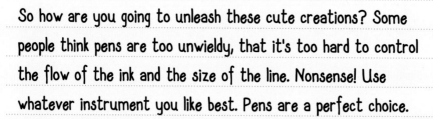

So how are you going to unleash these cute creations? Some people think pens are too unwieldy, that it's too hard to control the flow of the ink and the size of the line. Nonsense! Use whatever instrument you like best. Pens are a perfect choice.

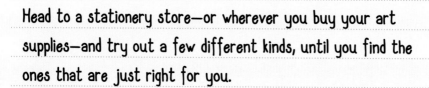

Head to a stationery store—or wherever you buy your art supplies—and try out a few different kinds, until you find the ones that are just right for you.

Now you're really ready to doodle. Have faith in the line your hand creates. Don't waver. Put the pen on the page with confidence and let your imagination guide the way. Even if you can't copy the illustrations in this book exactly, that's fine. They're just meant as guides or as inspiration as you find your own path into doodling.

Before you know it, you'll be doodling everywhere, on your notebooks and journals, on cards and notes. Personalize anything with your signature doodling style.

Happy doodling,
Kamo

How to Draw with a Ballpoint Pen

How should you hold the pen and what kind of lines should you make with it? It's time to learn the ropes, so copy the illustrations in this section until your page is filled with doodles.

Practicing Loopy Lines

Feeling loopy? Now it's time to step things up and add a little swirling motion to your lines. Keep your loops loose and flowing and see where they lead.

Loops below the line

Loops above the line

Big and small loops

Loops that stop halfway

Loops that resemble cursive script

A spiral forming a circle

A spiral going the other way

Combine them to form waves

Cloud

A cloud from a mass of curls

Use the loopy line to form a speech bubble

Examples

Cord

A curly line can be used to depict worry or anxiety

7

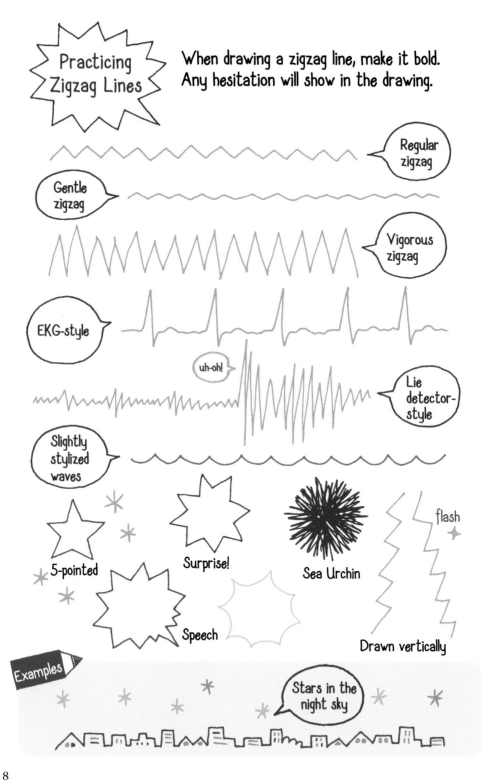

Practicing Zigzag Lines

When drawing a zigzag line, make it bold. Any hesitation will show in the drawing.

Regular zigzag

Gentle zigzag

Vigorous zigzag

EKG-style

uh-oh!

Lie detector-style

Slightly stylized waves

5-pointed

Surprise!

Sea Urchin

flash

Speech

Drawn vertically

Examples

Stars in the night sky

Practicing Dotted Lines

Create a trail when making a dotted line. Don't worry if the balance and spacing are a bit off: just do it!

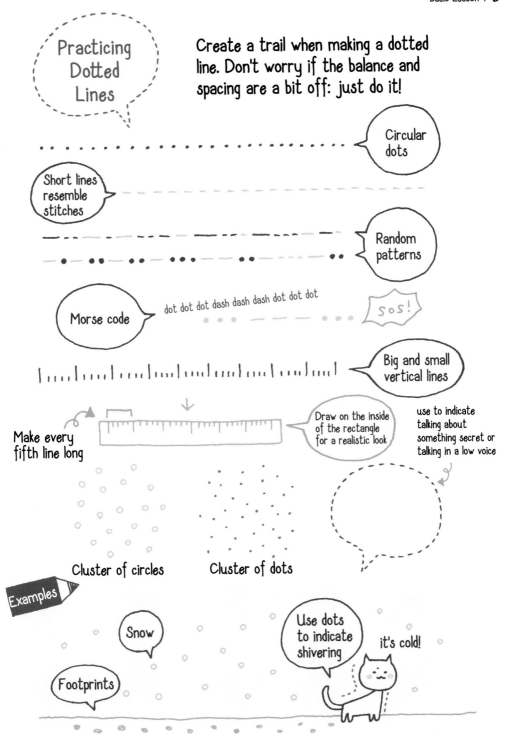

Circular dots

Short lines resemble stitches

Random patterns

Morse code

dot dot dot dash dash dash dot dot dot

SOS!

Big and small vertical lines

Make every fifth line long

Draw on the inside of the rectangle for a realistic look

use to indicate talking about something secret or talking in a low voice

Cluster of circles

Cluster of dots

Examples

Snow

Use dots to indicate shivering

it's cold!

Footprints

Using Circles

Even if described simply as a circle, a circular shape can take many forms. Think about drawings that incorporate any number of circular shapes.

Various circles

STEP 1

Illustrations you've probably done before that use circles

sun

smiley face

Ohm's law

bagel

half moons

flower

STEP 2

Illustrations that can be drawn nearly entirely from circles

donut

beads on a necklace

traffic light

STEP 3

○ + α

Illustrations using a circle and something else

bread

light bulb

boiled egg

Using Triangles

A triangle need not be precise, make it a little lopsided or off-balance for a less polished effect.

Various triangles

STEP 1

Illustrations you've probably done before that use triangles

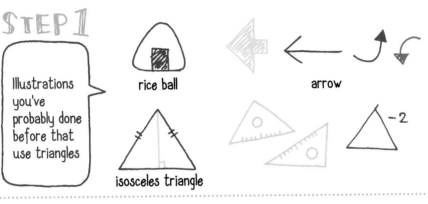

rice ball

arrow

isosceles triangle

−2

STEP 2

Illustrations that can be drawn nearly entirely from triangles

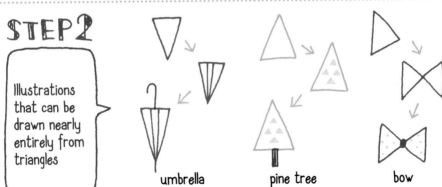

umbrella

pine tree

bow

STEP 3

△ + α

Illustrations using a triangle and something else

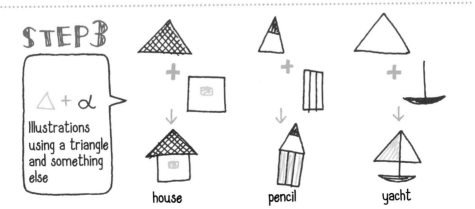

house

pencil

yacht

Using Squares

Their sharp corners make squares seem stiff, but with some tweaking, they're an essential, go-to shape.

Various squares

STEP 1

Illustrations you've probably done before that use squares

diamond

flag

letters and email

telephone number boxes

cross

square brackets

STEP 2

Illustrations that can be drawn nearly entirely from squares

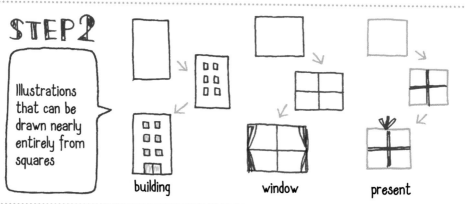

building

window

present

STEP 3

□ + α

Illustrations using a square and something else

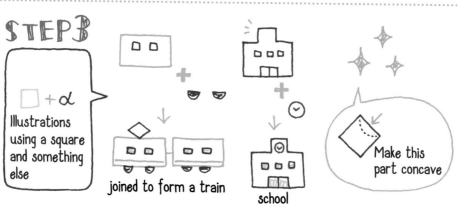

joined to form a train

school

Make this part concave

12

This is fun!

Oops! I messed up. Maybe it's this? Or this? Oh no...

No... .

When it's difficult to draw something in one go, use a pencil to make a faint draft

make sure to erase the draft lines

uncertain lines

switching direction

Sharp corners where the line switches direction make for an attractive drawing

try hard to draw the circular outline in one go

How to Trace

Trace this picture

tracing paper

Done!

Prepare tracing paper by drawing all over one side with pencil

you want to draw on a different piece of paper

you want to reverse the image

To reverse the image, turn the paper over

A

separate paper

turn over the tracing paper from step A so the side covered in pencil faces down and use a pencil to trace the image

The tracing paper from step A can be used multiple times

Trace over with a pen to finish up!

Coloring in with a Ballpoint Pen

Basic Lesson 2

Have you got a good grip on your pen? How do your lines look? Bold and confident, I hope. You're still learning the basics, but now it's time to take the next step. Practice these doodles, paying special attention to flow and flair.

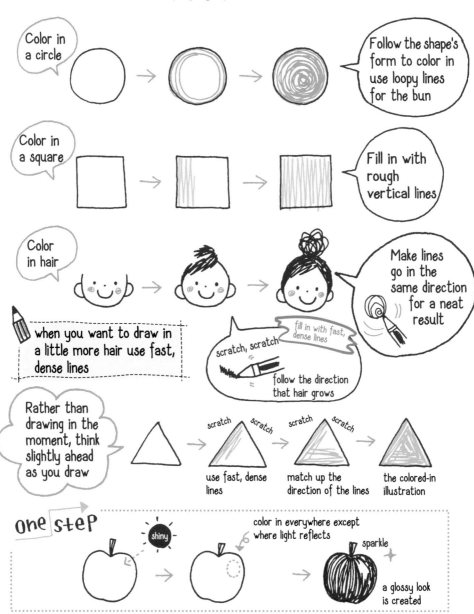

Color in a circle

Follow the shape's form to color in use loopy lines for the bun

Color in a square

Fill in with rough vertical lines

Color in hair

Make lines go in the same direction for a neat result

when you want to draw in a little more hair use fast, dense lines

scratch, scratch

fill in with fast, dense lines

follow the direction that hair grows

Rather than drawing in the moment, think slightly ahead as you draw

scratch scratch scratch scratch

use fast, dense lines

match up the direction of the lines

the colored-in illustration

one step

shiny

color in everywhere except where light reflects

sparkle

a glossy look is created

Using Lines to Color

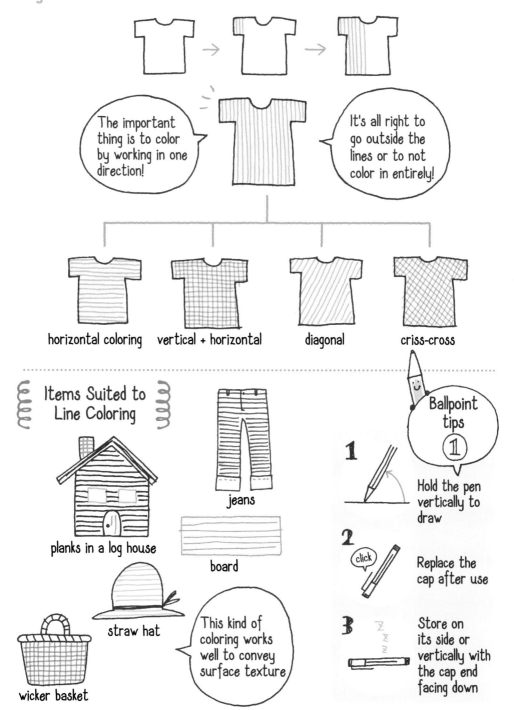

The important thing is to color by working in one direction!

It's all right to go outside the lines or to not color in entirely!

horizontal coloring

vertical + horizontal

diagonal

criss-cross

Items Suited to Line Coloring

planks in a log house

board

jeans

straw hat

wicker basket

This kind of coloring works well to convey surface texture

Ballpoint tips ①

1 Hold the pen vertically to draw

2 click Replace the cap after use

3 Store on its side or vertically with the cap end facing down

15

Using Dots to Color

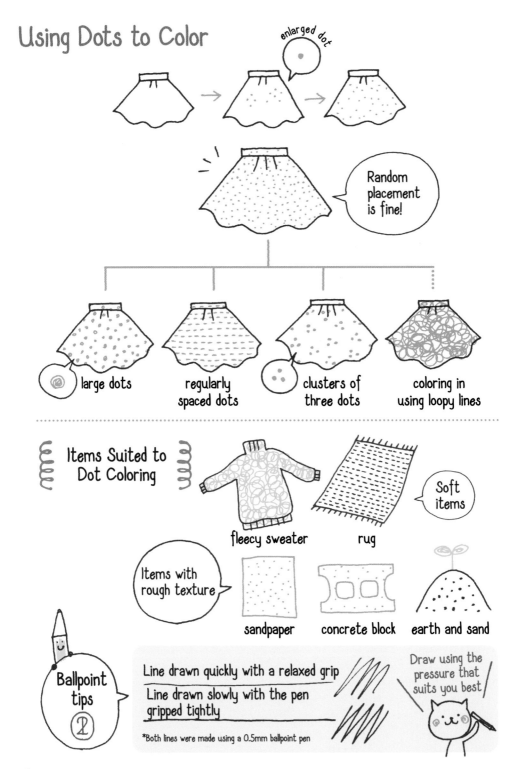

enlarged dot

Random placement is fine!

large dots

regularly spaced dots

clusters of three dots

coloring in using loopy lines

Items Suited to Dot Coloring

fleecy sweater

rug

Soft items

Items with rough texture

sandpaper

concrete block

earth and sand

Ballpoint tips ②

Line drawn quickly with a relaxed grip

Line drawn slowly with the pen gripped tightly

*Both lines were made using a 0.5mm ballpoint pen

Draw using the pressure that suits you best

Getting the Color Scheme Right

Color combinations

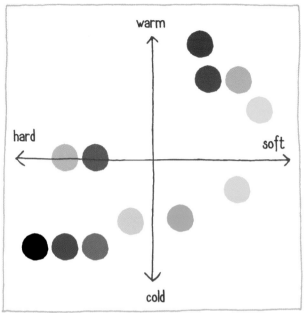

warm

hard ← → soft

cold

*Colors are subjective. This is for reference only.

Decide the Main Color and Add Others

	Monochrome	Two colors	Three colors
Navy			
Brown			
Gray			

Not sure what color to use?
Choose a main color and two colors that match it (if you have three colors you can draw just about anything)

France

Italy

Europe

Japan

China

Korea

Southeast Asia

Tropics

Snow country

Forest

Nautical

17

Ballpoint Pen Basics

Ink types

◎ Oil-based

The ink is viscous and doesn't bleed easily. As this is the classic type, a wide variety is available.

◎ Water-based

The ink has low viscosity, allowing for smooth drawing. It has the disadvantage of running if the paper gets wet.

◎ Gel

Combines the advantages of the oil and water types. Doesn't bleed easily and produces attractive color.

Various uses

◎ Pens for drawing on paper

The most traditional gel ink ballpoint pen. Produces attractive color when used on paper.

◎ Pens for drawing on photographs

Produces attractive color and doesn't run easily. Is water resistant and robust.

◎ Pens for drawing on dark paper

These ballpoint pens produce metallic colors that stand out on paper in dark colors such as black, dark brown, navy and so on.

◎ Pens for drawing on glass and plastic

Water-based pens that can draw on glass, plastic and metal.

◎ Pens for drawing on fabric

This type of pen doesn't run when used on fabric and the ink doesn't come out in the wash.

Pen tips come in thicknesses of 0.3, 0.5, 0.7, 1.0 and so on, but in this book we recommend 0.5

How to Use This Book

①

First, get accustomed to using a ballpoint pen by following Basic Lessons 1 and 2 from page 6 onward.

②

Practice depending on your goal, beginning with the categories you'd like to draw. Or, work toward a particular star level if you like.

③

If you still can't get things right no matter how many times you draw them, try practicing by tracing using the examples given.

LET'S DOODLE!

LESSON 1
Doodling on the Edges of Your Notebook Pages

Here we learn tips and tricks for drawing people, animals, plants and so on. Use little spaces such as the edge of a page in a notebook to bring out your originality.

Notebooks

The cover of your notebook covered in doodles? Why not. You can also scatter illustrations throughout the pages to match the subject, creating an original look.

Don't forget the reverse side!

Or how about a layered effect?

Business Cards

Business cards need to create an impression. Using a strong design sense, ruled lines and handwritten letters leads the way to a uniquely memorable card.

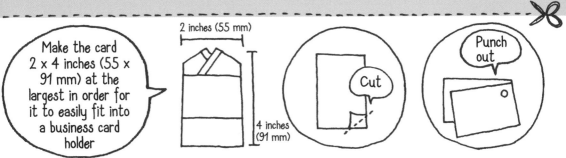

Make the card 2 x 4 inches (55 x 91 mm) at the largest in order for it to easily fit into a business card holder

2 inches (55 mm)

4 inches (91 mm)

Cut

Punch out

Hold it in front of your face when you're reading!

Close the book......

Book Covers

Use your favorite plain paper to create a book cover. Match the expression on the cover to the mood of the book and get ready to receive some attention!

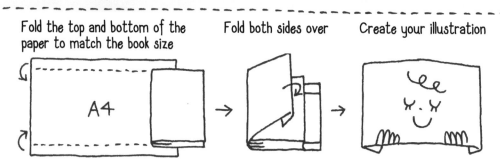

Fold the top and bottom of the paper to match the book size

A4

Fold both sides over

Create your illustration

Full-length
view......

Bookmarks

Why not create a handmade
bookmark too when you
make a book cover? Cut
out various shapes to
match the theme or mood
of the book, then decorate
them with ballpoint pen.

Template

×4

Use ballpoint pen to draw
illustrations, patterns and so on

Sandwich cord between the two
pieces of card and glue together

glue

1 Draw people multiple times in various ways

You'll want to get good at drawing people. The basics for drawing boys and girls are the same, so start by mastering them and then introduce changes to create original illustrations.

Start by trying to draw the face

Use jagged lines to indicate short hair

A wide neckline makes for a feminine look

Position the feet apart

Position the feet together

The differences between male and female can be easily expressed via small details

As long as the head and body are at an easy-to-draw ratio, it's O.K. A low head-to-body ratio makes for a cute look, while a higher number makes the figure look more adult

Altering the distance between the eyes

The position of the eyes significantly alters the look of a face

Work out what positioning is ideal for you

wide-set ←→ narrow-set

Having fun and feeling full of life

joy

The basic expression with the mouth open

When laughing, the eyes form >< shapes

Smiling eyes create a kind look

sadness

The ears, nose and mouth are all slightly lowered

A single teardrop

A profusion of tears

Eyes closed and downcast

anger

surprise

worry

Add symbols around the drawing

Make the eyes wide and bring out movement in the hair

Manga comics use lots of facial expressions so use them for reference

② Girls' appearances change depending on the outline, hairstyle and clothing

If you want to increase the numbers of different girls you can draw, change the outline of the face, hairstyle and clothing. Even changing just one of these should allow you to draw a variety of girls.

Variations in facial outline

Try changing the shape of the nose when you change the facial outline

long

basic

broad

triangular

basic face

bowl cut

curly

braids

center part

Variations in hairstyle

Variations in fashion

Make sure the left side of the kimono comes to the front

Fill in dark colors using lines so they work as an accent in the outfit

torso : legs = approx. 1:1

Adding a school uniform instantly creates a student

Give an adult woman a curved waist

3

Boys' appearances change depending on the outline, hairstyle and clothing, too

Variations of boys, too, can be created by changing the outline of the face, the hairstyle and the clothing. When adding color, choose a slightly dark shade.

Variations in facial outline

Emphasize the nose more than on girls or women

long and narrow

basic

broad

triangular

basic

face

short

curly

messy ends

beard and glasses

Variations in hairstyles

28

Variations in fashion

The kimono crosses with the left side on top for both men and women

When layering color, use the light color and then the dark

The torso : legs ratio is 1:1, the same as for females

Use lines when coloring in a dark garment.

Make sure to define the width of the shoulders for a firm look

29

4

Keep placement in mind for people of different ages

When drawing people of different ages—from babies and children to old men and women—it's important to keep the placement of their body parts in mind.

baby   child

Make the face round!

A baby's height is about twice the size of its head

A child looks cute with a head about a third of its height

The basics are the same for children

Make the face broader than that of an adult

The eyes, nose and mouth are all positioned slightly low on the face

Babies and children can be drawn the same way whether they are male or female. Differentiate between them by using accessories, colors and so on

A wide gap between the eyes creates a childlike look (see page 25)

(see page 25)

Variations in pose

toys

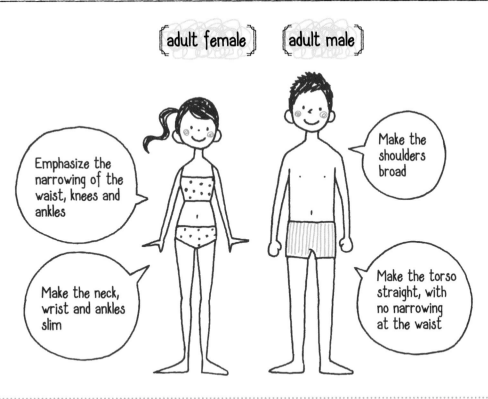

[adult female] [adult male]

Emphasize the narrowing of the waist, knees and ankles

Make the shoulders broad

Make the neck, wrist and ankles slim

Make the torso straight, with no narrowing at the waist

[old lady] [old man]

The low bun is a typical style for an older woman

Create a calm facial expression

This type of hat is favored by older men

Leaving gaps in the coloring creates the look of gray hair

Make the back rounded

Spectacles might be a nice touch

Make the waist thick

31

5 Pay attention to the joints depending on the direction figures are facing and their movement

Once you've practiced drawing upright figures, try changing the angle and movements. Compare the drawing with your own body.

Basics of direction

Make the nose stick out when drawing in profile

For right-handed people, it's easiest to draw figures facing left, while for left-handed people, it's easiest to draw figures facing right

reverse

basic figure

Subtle angles can be depicted through positioning (make the ear in the foreground larger than the one at the back)

When you reverse the image, watch out for which side the hair is parted on

TIP

Draw the figure facing the direction you are comfortable with and then trace it to easily reverse the image!

Basics of drawing people

People's joints bend in a set direction so if you are aware of this you can draw any pose you like

Stick to the basics when drawing animals

6

When drawing familiar animals such as rabbits, cats and so on, the basics are the same for each animal. Master the basics so you can draw all kinds of animals.

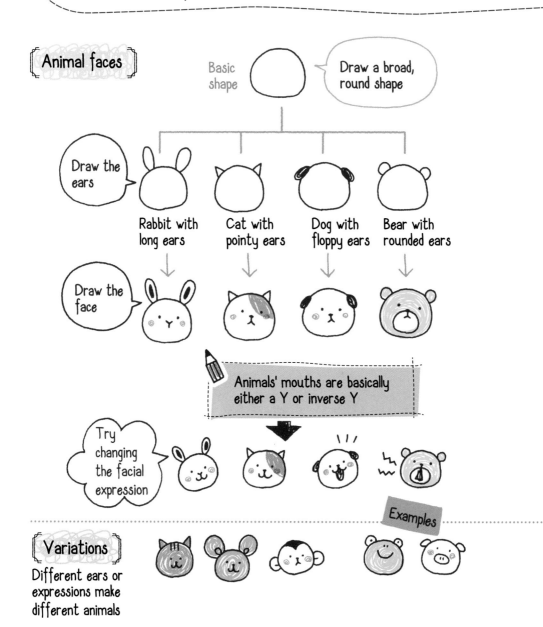

Animal faces

Basic shape — Draw a broad, round shape

Draw the ears

Rabbit with long ears | Cat with pointy ears | Dog with floppy ears | Bear with rounded ears

Draw the face

Animals' mouths are basically either a Y or inverse Y

Try changing the facial expression

Examples

Variations

Different ears or expressions make different animals

Animal faces (in profile)

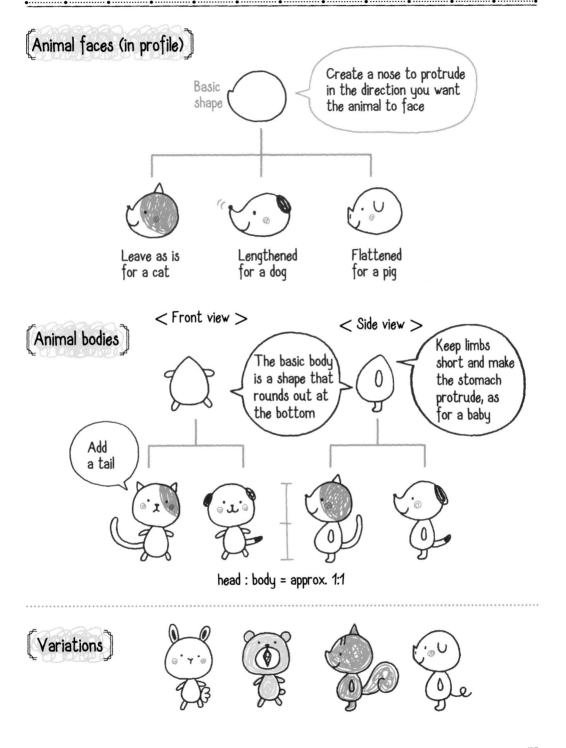

Basic shape

Create a nose to protrude in the direction you want the animal to face

Leave as is for a cat

Lengthened for a dog

Flattened for a pig

Animal bodies

< Front view >

< Side view >

The basic body is a shape that rounds out at the bottom

Keep limbs short and make the stomach protrude, as for a baby

Add a tail

head : body = approx. 1:1

Variations

A dog is the standard four-legged animal

Once you've mastered how to draw animals on page 34, have a go at drawing man's best friend. Pay particular attention to the adorable movements unique to dogs.

Let's have a go at developing the basic dog on the previous page

[Developing dogs]

When you want to make the drawings more like characters

When you want to make the drawings more like real animals

Add movement

Add the body

Add clothing

Draw them on all fours

Animals' characteristic movements are easier to express when they are on all fours. See the page to the right for examples

Make the drawing even simpler...

...it's still a dog!

Dogs

woof!

Think of the body as a triangle

Draw two legs extending out at both the front and back to create a stretched-out appearance

sitting (side view)

leaping

It's O.K. to simplify legs that are not visible

lolling around

sitting (front view)

rear view

The front and rear legs are clearly depicted in a neat line

Types of dogs

Hair for a poodle

Draw big ears to create a Papillon

Elongate the body for a dachshund

Focus on characteristics to the point of overemphasis to get just the right effect

For larger dogs, increase the size of the body section

37

Bring out cats' lithe, fluid movements

8 Use the same instructions on page 34, only this time to draw a cat. Make the movements slightly looser than that of a dog for a realistic look.

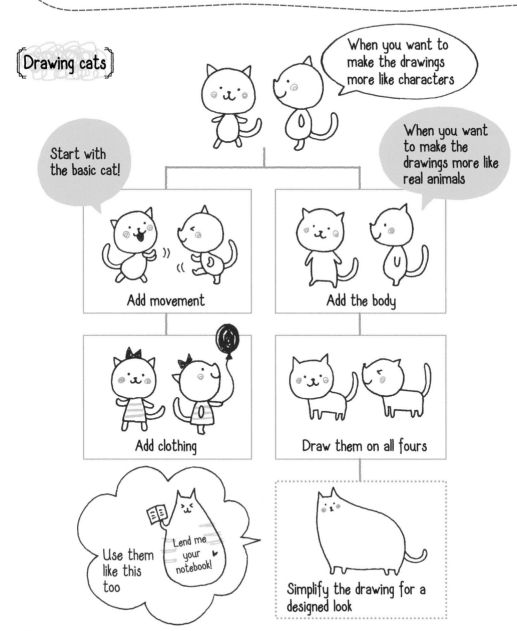

Drawing cats

When you want to make the drawings more like characters

Start with the basic cat!

When you want to make the drawings more like real animals

Add movement

Add the body

Add clothing

Draw them on all fours

Use them like this too

Lend me your notebook!

Simplify the drawing for a designed look

Cat behavior

Show the line of the back

Make the line looser and more curved than that of a dog for a more catlike appearance

Sitting (side view)

If you are having difficulty drawing the legs, simplify things by giving them the look of being tucked out of sight

sniff

Sitting (front view)

Meow!

rear view

ZZZ

Make the shoulders smooth and narrow

Types of cats

White socks

Make adult bodies much bigger than kittens'

Tabby

Many variations can be created simply by changing the pattern of the cat's coat

Persian

39

9 Understand an animal's characteristics

Use your practice drawing dogs and cats as a base for drawing other animals. It's surprisingly easy to depict each animal if you incorporate its particular characteristics.

Horses and similar animals

< face >

For animals similar to horses, it is easiest to draw them from the side

< body >

← neck

← torso

2   2

Add stripes

Make the main lines the color of the animal. It doesn't matter if you don't color in the whole animal

Length

Make a few changes and add two humps to create a camel

40

Animals with rounded bodies

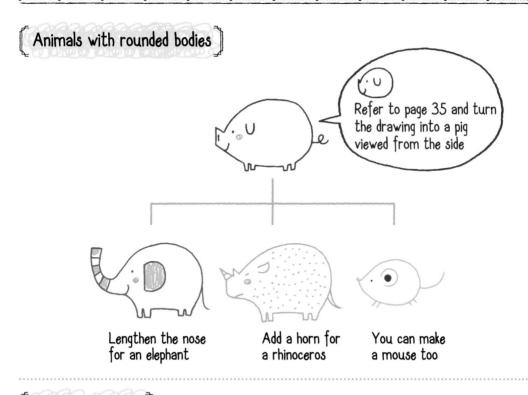

Refer to page 35 and turn the drawing into a pig viewed from the side

Lengthen the nose for an elephant

Add a horn for a rhinoceros

You can make a mouse too

Other applications

The ears and nose are key

Big legs

Thick tail

Create a bold mane

Lengthen the limbs to overemphasize the movements

Animals' particular characteristics make them easy to draw

Use the facial expression to help bring out cuteness

10 Use a circle as the foundation to draw a bird

Drawing a circle as the foundation for a bird makes for an adorable result. Exaggerate its characteristics just like with other animals.

Bird basics

Add wings

Start with a circle when drawing birds, too

A slight diagonal angle makes drawing easier

Make the wings look as if they're flapping. It's O.K. not to draw the feet

inside a nest

eggs

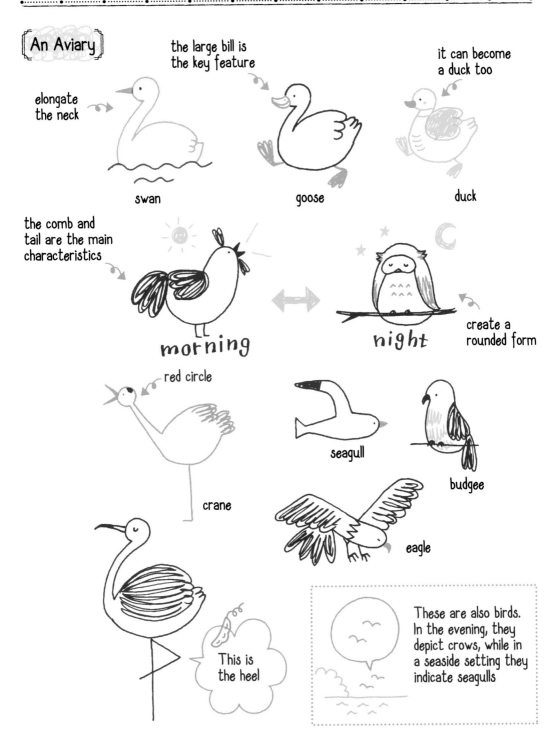

An Aviary

the large bill is
the key feature

it can become
a duck too

elongate
the neck

swan

goose

duck

the comb and
tail are the main
characteristics

morning

night

create a
rounded form

red circle

seagull

budgee

crane

eagle

This is
the heel

These are also birds.
In the evening, they
depict crows, while in
a seaside setting they
indicate seagulls

43

11 Use patterns to create variations in sea creatures

Sea creatures are patterned in all kinds of ways. Make them colorful to recreate the look of an aquarium.

[Fish basics]

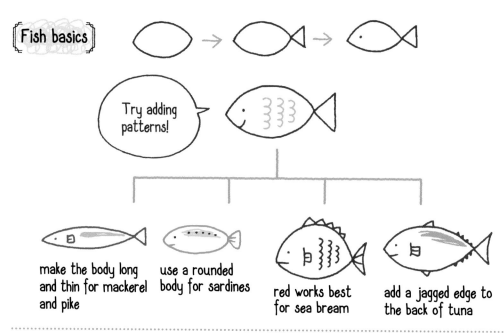

Try adding patterns!

make the body long and thin for mackerel and pike

use a rounded body for sardines

red works best for sea bream

add a jagged edge to the back of tuna

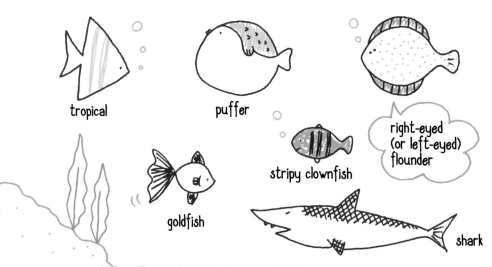

tropical

puffer

right-eyed (or left-eyed) flounder

stripy clownfish

goldfish

shark

squid

Squid have 10 legs and octopuses have eight, but it's fine to simplify them

octopus

side view

crab

shell 1

shell 2

Other sea creatures

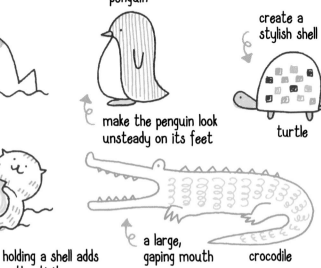

penguin

create a stylish shell

whale

water spouts from the back

make the penguin look unsteady on its feet

turtle

otter

holding a shell adds authenticity

a large, gaping mouth

crocodile

12 Know an insect's structure to get it right

Have you ever looked at an insect closely? They're familiar yet unfamiliar at the same time. With three parts to their tiny bodies, drawing them can sometimes be tricky.

Bug basics

Insects' bodies are divided into the head, chest and abdomen sections

The legs sprout from the chest section

head

chest

abdomen

a stag beetle with a horn

a dragonfly's head is basically all eyes

make the chest section fuzzy

give a grasshopper long antennas

The wings also sprout from the chest section

For insects with particular characteristics, it's fine not to be too fussy about the head, chest and abdomen sections

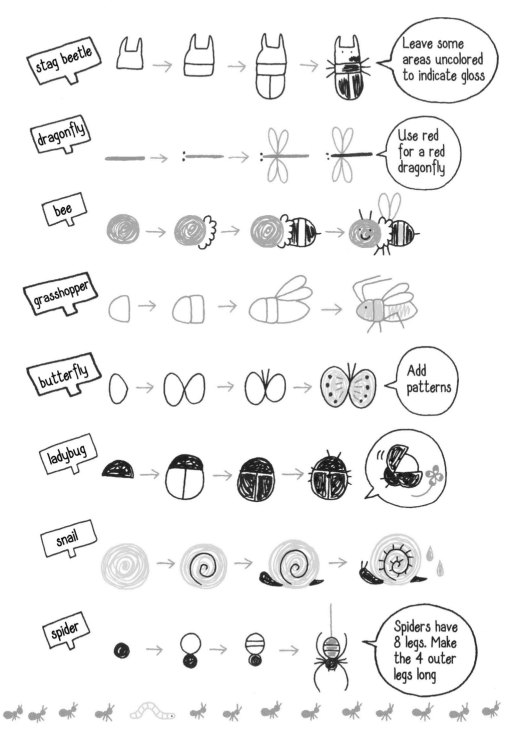

Consider how to link the zodiac motifs

13 The motifs for the zodiac signs are super cute and you're sure to want to draw them often. Add a star to each one or some other unifying feature as you draw them.

[The twelve signs]

48

When drawing items of the same type, find a common link to unify them. In this case, a star has been incorporated into each illustration

Libra

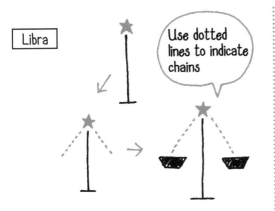

Use dotted lines to indicate chains

Scorpio

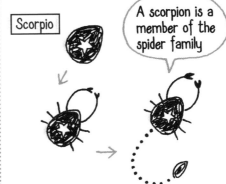

A scorpion is a member of the spider family

Sagittarius

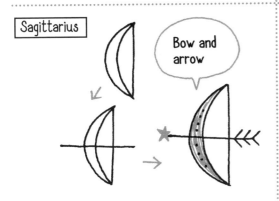

Bow and arrow

Capricorn

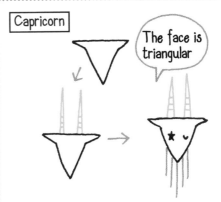

The face is triangular

Aquarius

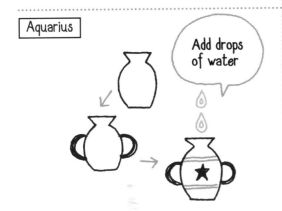

Add drops of water

Pisces

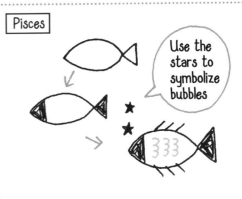

Use the stars to symbolize bubbles

Add flair to the Chinese zodiac

Give Chinese zodiac signs a stylized look when adding them to New Years' cards and other greetings.

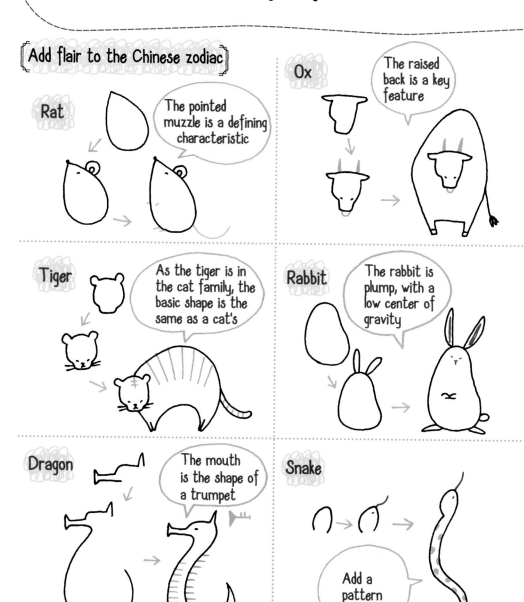

Add flair to the Chinese zodiac

Rat — The pointed muzzle is a defining characteristic

Ox — The raised back is a key feature

Tiger — As the tiger is in the cat family, the basic shape is the same as a cat's

Rabbit — The rabbit is plump, with a low center of gravity

Dragon — The mouth is the shape of a trumpet

Snake — Add a pattern

Make the head of the animal small and the body large for a mature air. Round eyes are cute, while narrow eyes create a slightly robotic look

Horse

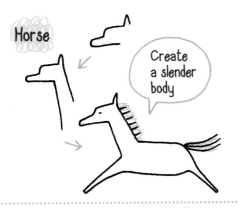

Create a slender body

Sheep

Make the coat curly

Monkey

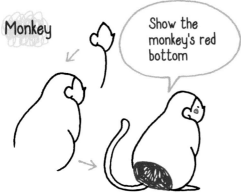

Show the monkey's red bottom

Rooster

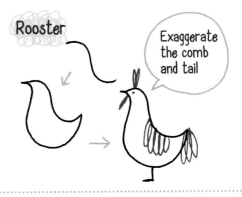

Exaggerate the comb and tail

Dog

Rather than a pet, create the look of a guard dog

Boar

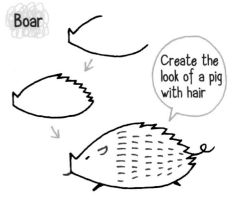

Create the look of a pig with hair

15 Use loops and jagged lines for leaves on trees

Plants are another popular theme. Notice how various types of trees can be expressed depending on how the ballpoint pen is used to create color.

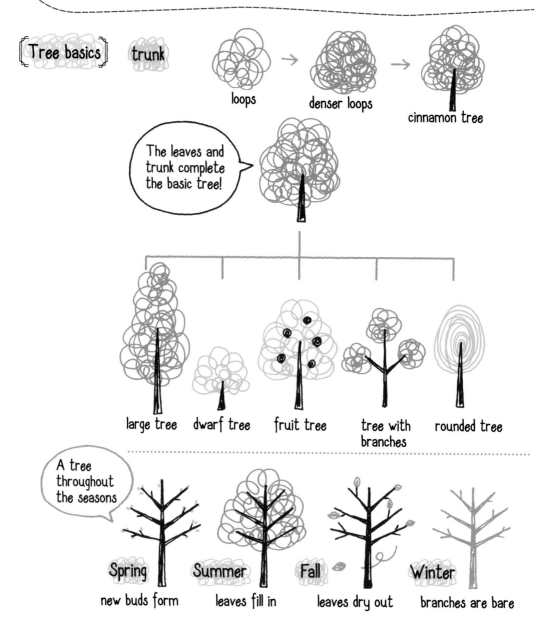

Tree basics trunk

loops

denser loops

cinnamon tree

The leaves and trunk complete the basic tree!

large tree dwarf tree fruit tree tree with branches rounded tree

A tree throughout the seasons

Spring Summer Fall Winter

new buds form leaves fill in leaves dry out branches are bare

52

Types of trees

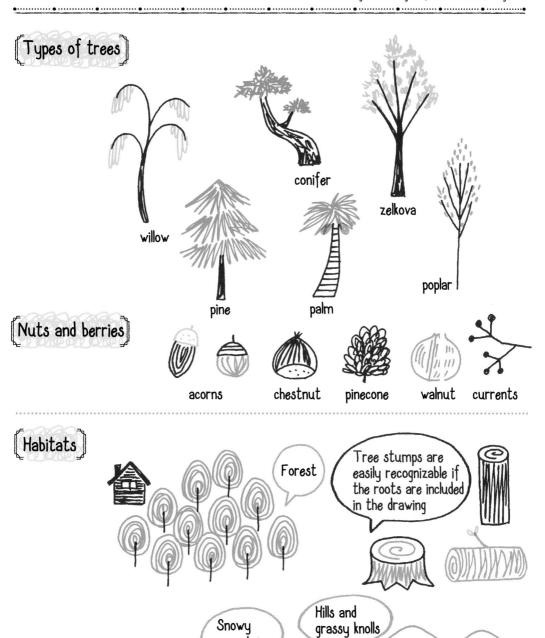

willow

conifer

zelkova

poplar

pine

palm

Nuts and berries

acorns   chestnut   pinecone   walnut   currents

Habitats

Forest

Tree stumps are easily recognizable if the roots are included in the drawing

Snowy mountains

Hills and grassy knolls

Use color to create gorgeous flowers

16 If you're not yet skilled at drawing people or animals, have a go at drawing flowers. Get to know the basics in order to create colorful illustrations.

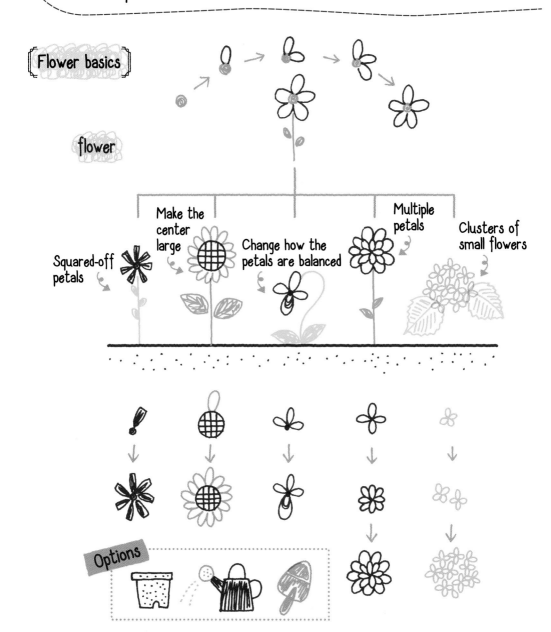

Flower basics

flower

Squared-off petals

Make the center large

Change how the petals are balanced

Multiple petals

Clusters of small flowers

Options

54

Types of flowers

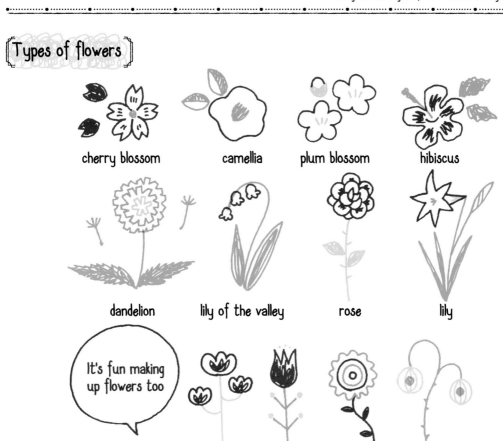

cherry blossom   camellia   plum blossom   hibiscus

dandelion   lily of the valley   rose   lily

It's fun making up flowers too

Ground cover

Leaves

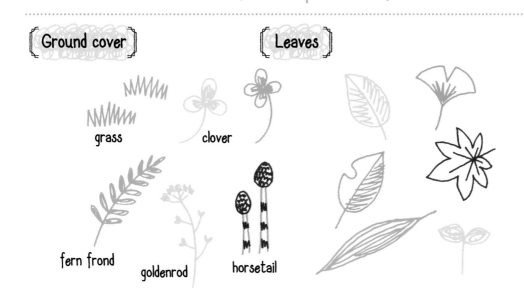

grass   clover

fern frond   goldenrod   horsetail

17 Depict various water and sky conditions

Water can appear in various forms. Similarly, the sky looks different depending on the time of day. Take note of their characteristics to add a touch of realism to your drawings.

Water, Water Everywhere!

Seaside sights

In the sky

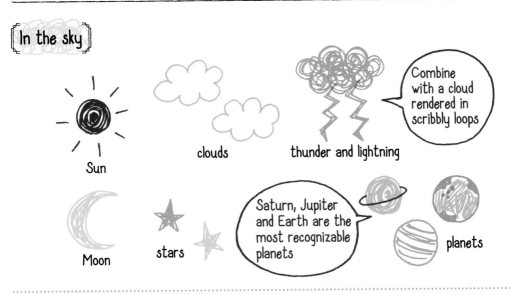

Sun

clouds

thunder and lightning

Combine with a cloud rendered in scribbly loops

Moon

stars

Saturn, Jupiter and Earth are the most recognizable planets

planets

Combinations

blue sky

night sky

Even just coloring in rough lines can suggest the sky

sundown

sunrise

rainbow

Seven colors

Sky sights

18 Why not show a cross-section when drawing fruit?

Usually, when drawing fruit, the tendency is to depict the form as a whole, but some fruits lend themselves to being shown as cross-sections. If you're not used to drawing them, practice with these.

Fruit fundamentals   Exterior   Cross-section

apple
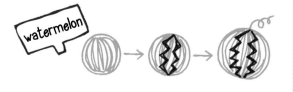   

watermelon
   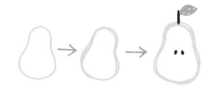

tangerine

banana
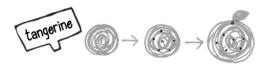   

pear
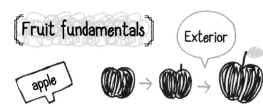   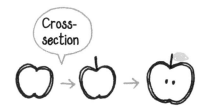

kiwi

58

Other fruits

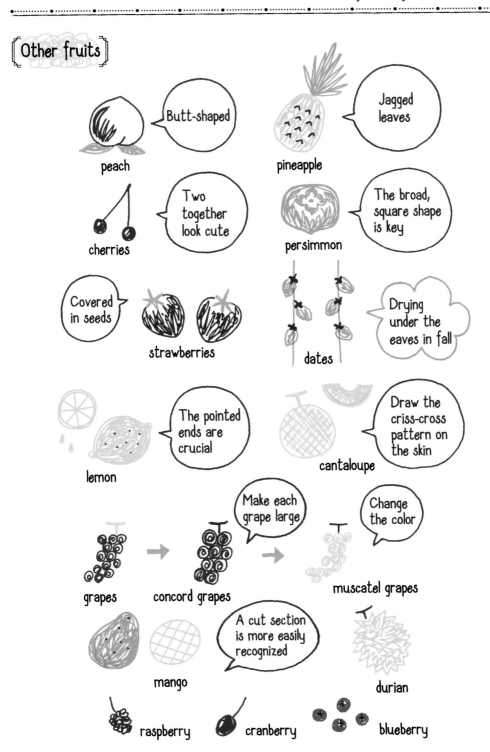

peach — Butt-shaped

pineapple — Jagged leaves

cherries — Two together look cute

persimmon — The broad, square shape is key

strawberries — Covered in seeds

dates — Drying under the eaves in fall

lemon — The pointed ends are crucial

cantaloupe — Draw the criss-cross pattern on the skin

grapes → concord grapes — Make each grape large → muscatel grapes — Change the color

mango — A cut section is more easily recognized

durian

raspberry   cranberry   blueberry

19 Color with care when drawing vegetables

Use different methods of adding color to depict vegetables. Try drawing a few of them on something like a menu.

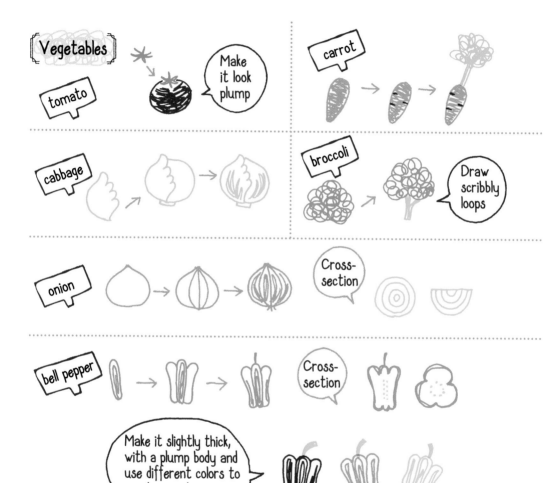

Vegetables

tomato — Make it look plump

carrot

cabbage

broccoli — Draw scribbly loops

onion — Cross-section

bell pepper — Cross-section

Make it slightly thick, with a plump body and use different colors to create variety

pumpkin and squash — Cross-section

Other vegetables

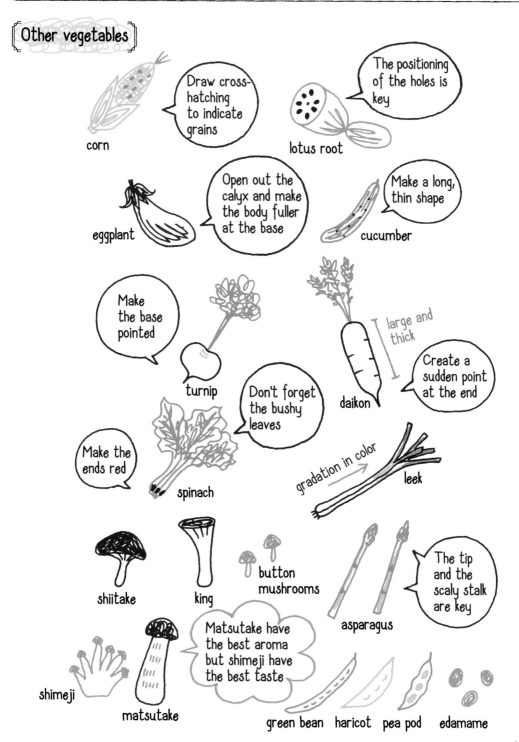

Draw cross-hatching to indicate grains

corn

The positioning of the holes is key

lotus root

Open out the calyx and make the body fuller at the base

eggplant

Make a long, thin shape

cucumber

Make the base pointed

turnip

large and thick

daikon

Create a sudden point at the end

Don't forget the bushy leaves

Make the ends red

spinach

gradation in color

leek

shiitake

king

button mushrooms

The tip and the scaly stalk are key

asparagus

Matsutake have the best aroma but shimeji have the best taste

shimeji

matsutake

green bean   haricot   pea pod   edamame

Tracing Time

Place thin paper over the top of the illustrations featured so far and trace them as many times as you like.

LET'S DOODLE!

LESSON 2

Gift Decoration Doodles That Show How Much You Care

Dress up a gift with your own doodles.
Personalize your presents to add that
extra touch of thoughtfulness.

Paper Bags

When giving
someone a present
or returning something
you've borrowed, deliver warm
feelings as well by drawing
illustrations on the paper bag.

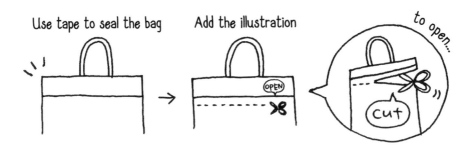

Use tape to seal the bag → Add the illustration

OPEN

to open...

cut

64

Labels

These labels can be stuck on glass jars filled with jam or any homemade treat. Draw something cute that will show the contents in a glance. These also work well on gifts.

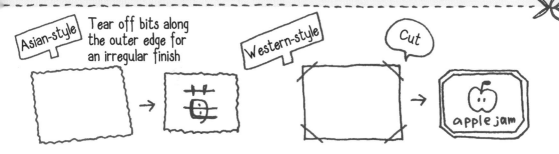

Nametags

Use handmade nametags to label your stuff for school, home, wherever. A fabric marker or pen allows you to doodle directly onto your personal items.

Draw on fabric

These pens don't drag on the fabric but create a very smooth, flowing line

⚠️ The ink may transfer to items under the fabric so make sure to place a cloth under it

Wrapping Paper

Wrapping done at a store may be attractive, but something seems to be missing. Create handmade wrapping paper by drawing on the packaging. This is the perfect complement when giving handmade gifts.

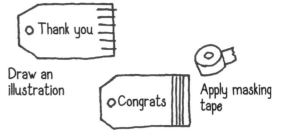

Template

Draw an illustration

o Thank you

oCongrats

Apply masking tape

67

20 Keep dimension in mind when drawing food

Most food, particularly when packaged, appears more appetizing when it is drawn to look three-dimensional rather than flat.

[Basics of 2D and 3D] Depicted as flat, items are cute and resemble symbols, while dimensional drawings are seen as more skilled. Intentionally breaking down a 3D drawing slightly makes for a stylish look

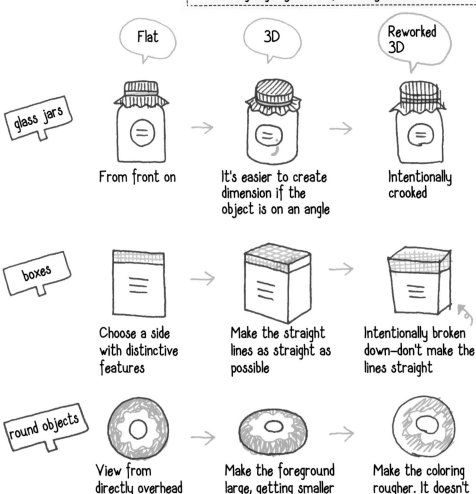

Flat

3D

Reworked 3D

glass jars

From front on

It's easier to create dimension if the object is on an angle

Intentionally crooked

boxes

Choose a side with distinctive features

Make the straight lines as straight as possible

Intentionally broken down—don't make the lines straight

round objects

View from directly overhead

Make the foreground large, getting smaller toward the back

Make the coloring rougher. It doesn't have to be neat

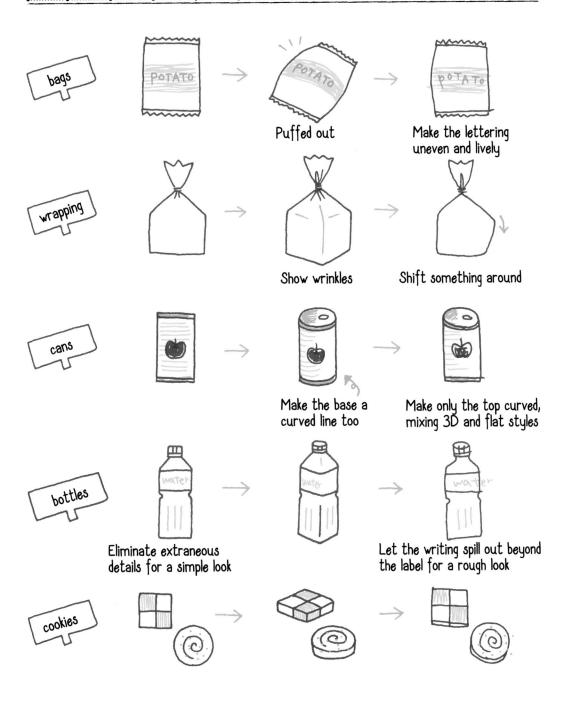

bags

Puffed out

Make the lettering uneven and lively

wrapping

Show wrinkles

Shift something around

cans

Make the base a curved line too

Make only the top curved, mixing 3D and flat styles

bottles

Eliminate extraneous details for a simple look

Let the writing spill out beyond the label for a rough look

cookies

21

Add plenty of color to bread and baked goods

It's nice to add little illustrations when sharing a batch of handmade cookies or home-baked bread with friends. Make sure to use lots of color.

⌜Breads and cookies⌟

bread rolls

Make the burnt sections slightly dark

loaf of bread

Add small dots to the surface

bagels

Use different colors to distinguish the types

baguettes

A la Parisienne

croissants

Show how the pastry wraps around

melon bread

Use criss-cross lines like on melon skin

sandwiches

Use green for lettuce, pink for ham and so on

pancakes

slices of cake

This can become cheese too

torte

cupcakes

cakes

jelly rolls

Ice cream

[Other sweet treats]

candy variations

Draw the paper wrapping too when drawing a block of chocolate

Make good use of line when drawing cooked food and drinks

Observe the defining features of cooked food and drinks. Don't simply color in the whole drawing, but use line effectively and then add color for an adorable result.

[Cooked]

pasta

When drawing multiples, position one on a different angle

Change the color of the pasta or sauce to create variations

omelettes

Draw ketchup on if you like

pizza

Cutting out a slice works well

hamburger

Add color for a vibrant look

steak

Bring out thickness for a sense of luxury

egg dishes

Adjust the balance of colors

salads

Use three colors

rice

miso soup

fish

tempura

yakitori

ramen

udon noodles

soba noodles

coffee

black tea

drawing ice

green tea

water

Note the form of cooking utensils and cutlery

They may be a bit complicated in shape, but their cuteness makes cooking utensils and cutlery tempting subjects for illustration.
Looking at them carefully to understand their form is the first step.

plates

cups

glasses

knives

forks

spoons

chopsticks

Add a chopstick holder

napkin

butter knife

Drawing the side view is easiest

Chinese soup spoon

condiments

24 Keep line and surface in mind when drawing

Pay attention to the surfaces of the things you use everyday. How can you use your doodle lines to create texture and contour?

Using line creates a simple look, while filling in surfaces makes for a more solid impression. It's fine to combine the two, but consider the overall balance and add or remove color as needed

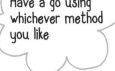

Have a go using whichever method you like

[Surface, Texture and Line]

Line

Surface

Line and surface

cotton spool

Gives the impression of fine thread

Gives the impression of thick thread

Combining line and surface creates a stylized look

hat

Light for summer

Heavier for winter

A band around the hat stands out and pulls the look together

person

For a quick, light touch

Adding more color makes the drawing

The entire surface area of the hair is filled in while line is used for the outline. Most people in this book are drawn in this way

See page 24 for how to draw people!

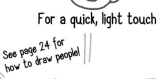

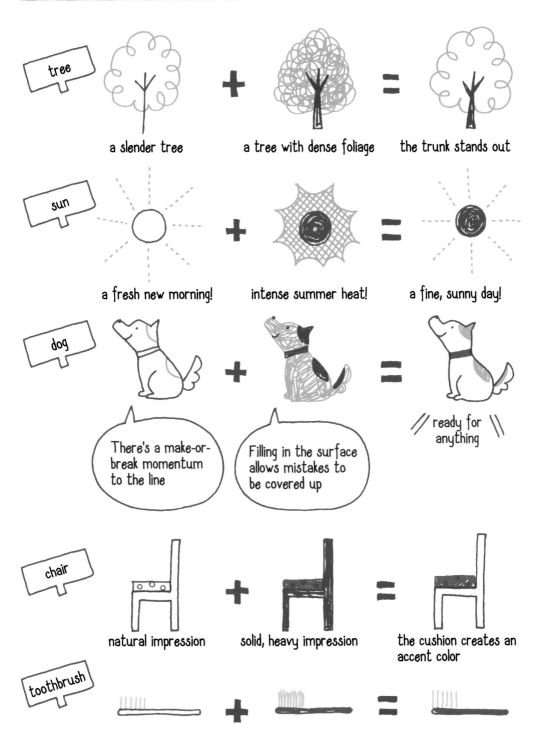

tree

a slender tree + a tree with dense foliage = the trunk stands out

sun

a fresh new morning! + intense summer heat! = a fine, sunny day!

dog

+ = // ready for anything \\

There's a make-or-break momentum to the line

Filling in the surface allows mistakes to be covered up

chair

natural impression + solid, heavy impression = the cushion creates an accent color

toothbrush

+ =

Simplify the shapes of handicraft items

25

Drawings of craft supplies add a personal touch to handmade presents. A doodle instantly boosts the appeal of the gift item.

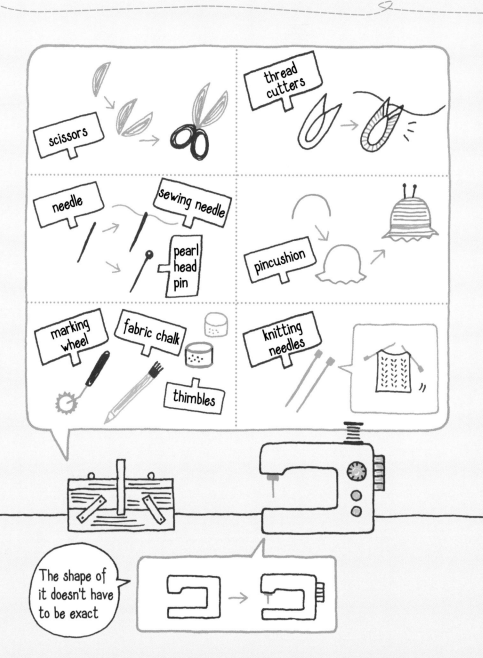

scissors

thread cutters

needle

sewing needle

pearl head pin

pincushion

marking wheel

fabric chalk

thimbles

knitting needles

The shape of it doesn't have to be exact

sewing machine thread

hand-sewing thread

stitches

lace

buttons

wool

fabric variations

Draw the plate of the iron

Come up with all kinds of patterns!

26 Take note of straight lines when drawing stationery

These everyday stationery objects are used at school, in the office and at home. The key to drawing them is making the straight lines rough.

notebook

dictionary

Make it thick and solid

pencils

mechanical pencil

The tip of the pen is the key feature

pen

eraser

School

Consider color combos when drawing fashion accessories

Vibrantly colored fashion accessories command attention with their bold patterns and textured surfaces. Add them to a card or note, choosing items that reflect the recipient's personality and taste.

27

purses and handbags

wallets

Show bills sticking out

glasses

watches

men's

large

wide

women's

small

narrow

Men's

Make them look sturdy

Stripes in the knot run in the opposite direction from the stripes in the body of the tie

28 Tie the look together when drawing interiors

When drawing interiors and their furnishings, it's important to create the sense that they all fit together. Draw them to your own taste, in colors that you like.

84

microwave → ding!

fridge → retro style

washing machine → drum

Pare back detail to simplify household electrical goods

chairs

Even if it only has two legs, as long as it resembles a chair it's O.K.

ornamental plants

Bring out the sparkle of cosmetics

(29) There's something alluring about the shiny packaging of cosmetics.
Try to recreate it in your drawing.

Get the shape right when drawing modes of transport

We see various types of transport every day, but they're hard to get right when drawing. Practice them over and over until you can draw them easily.

airplane

ship

car

bus

train

Draw wheels outside the body of the vehicle for a car, inside for a train

88

Tracing Time

Place thin paper over the top of the illustrations featured

so far and trace them as many times as you like.

LET'S DOODLE!

LESSON 3
Adding Cute Colors to Planners and Scrapbooks

Use doodles to bring diaries, scrapbooks and planners to life. Record a special memory or indicate an upcoming event with your own special touches.

Diaries

Adding cute illustrations to fun events you've scheduled will make each day even more enjoyable.

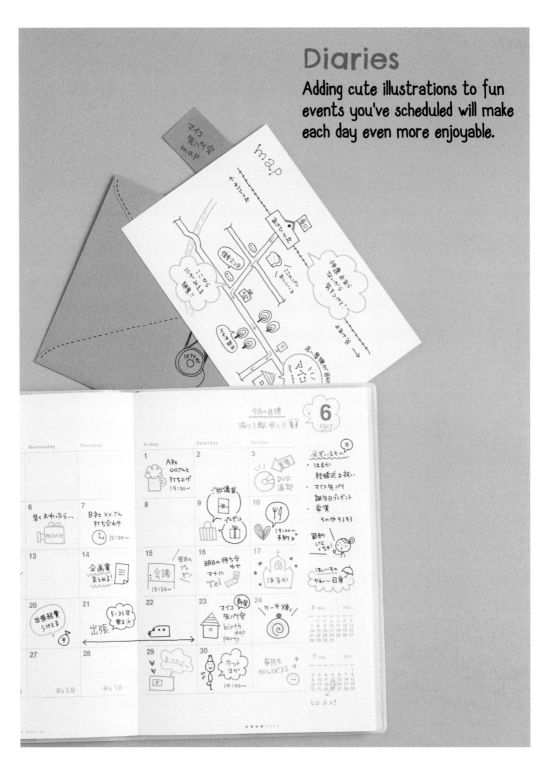

Calendars

Calendars are made for doodles. All that white space! Add drawings to indicate important appointments, events, holidays and celebrations.

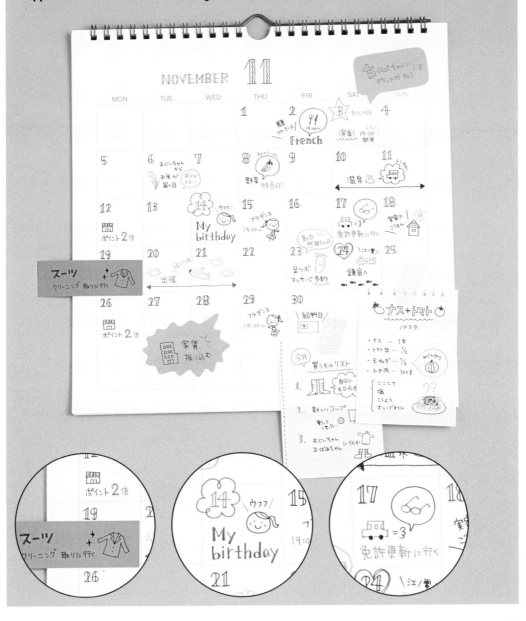

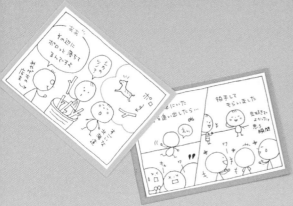

Sketchbooks

Fill your travel journal with drawings of sights and scenes from your trip. Cover the whole page with illustrations to capture these vacation memories.

Photos

Use illustrations to decorate photos, too. Your friends will love to decorate photos as well.

These pens can draw on photos

The surface is shiny, so draw slowly in order for the ink to spread smoothly

⚠ The color will be more defined once dry (especially white)

Place importance on the setting when drawing events

Decorate your organizer with the events of the season. Simplify human figures as much as possible and emphasize the setting.

Spring

Spring semester

Graduation

Spring birthday

Mother's Day

Cherry blossom viewing

Company initiation ceremony

Summer

Beach time

Hiking

4th of July

BBQs

Summer festivals

TICKETS

96

Make the people simple stick figures!

Fall

""" Picnics """

Sporting events

Harvest time

Cultural festival

Fall gallery season

Winter

Fun in the snow

Kite flying

Skiing

Ice skating

32 Use icons in drawings to represent events

For the doodles and drawings in your planner, it's important to make them simple and easily identifiable—like icons, in other words.

Spring

Graduation

School

Kite flying

Dolls

Mother's Day

Father's Day

Summer

Stars

Fireworks

Festivals

Traveling

Visits

Fall

Fall foliage

Harvest festivals

Halloween

Autumn vegetables

Winter

Christmas

New Year's Day

LovE

Valentine's Day

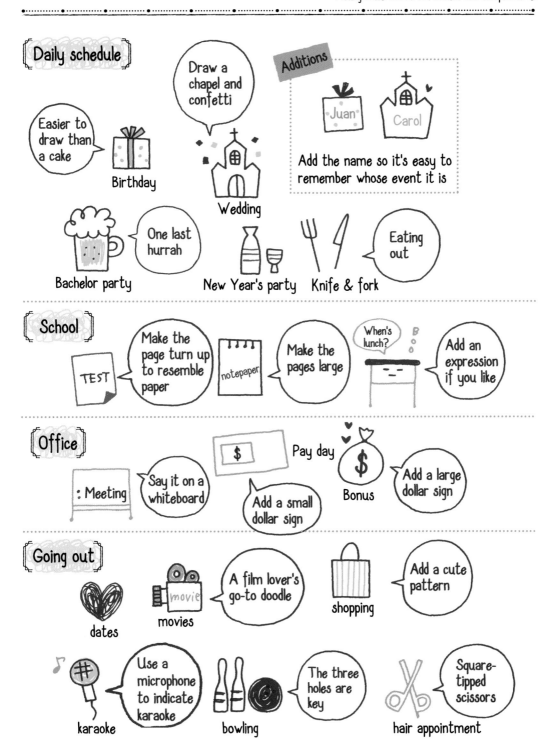

Daily schedule

Easier to draw than a cake

Birthday

Draw a chapel and confetti

Wedding

Additions

Juan

Carol

Add the name so it's easy to remember whose event it is

One last hurrah

Bachelor party

New Year's party

Knife & fork

Eating out

School

TEST

Make the page turn up to resemble paper

notepaper

Make the pages large

When's lunch?

Add an expression if you like

Office

: Meeting

Say it on a whiteboard

$

Pay day

Add a small dollar sign

$

Bonus

Add a large dollar sign

Going out

dates

movie

movies

A film lover's go-to doodle

shopping

Add a cute pattern

karaoke

Use a microphone to indicate karaoke

bowling

The three holes are key

hair appointment

Square-tipped scissors

33 Use color and focus on defining characteristics to depict school subjects

It's fun to add illustrations to your school timetable. Make them stand out and try drawing them on the notebooks for each subject, too.

Foreign language

The vertical lines of text are the key feature. Make the book really thick

Math

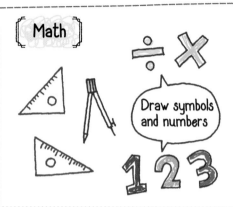

Draw symbols and numbers

Science

There's a lot of cool items used for science experiments

Social studies

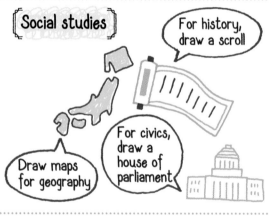

For history, draw a scroll

Draw maps for geography

For civics, draw a house of parliament

English

Add patterns to letters of the alphabet

Speaking

Gym

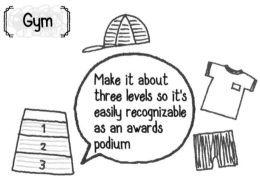

Make it about three levels so it's easily recognizable as an awards podium

Shop

Tools are easily recognizable

Home economics

The stitch-like decorations are cute

Calligraphy

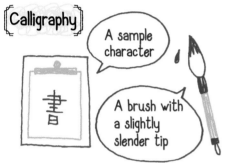

A sample character

A brush with a slightly slender tip

Art

A slightly plump paintbrush

Music

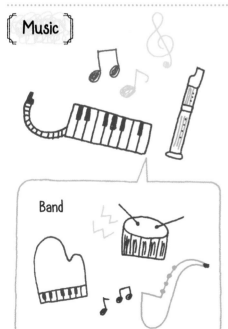

Band

Clubs

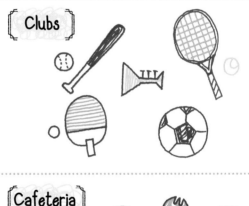

Cafeteria

A spoon that doubles as a fork

Lunch

Ease of use is top priority for maps!

34

Are you moving? Having a party? Add a map to your announcement or invite—just be sure it's accurate.

The basics

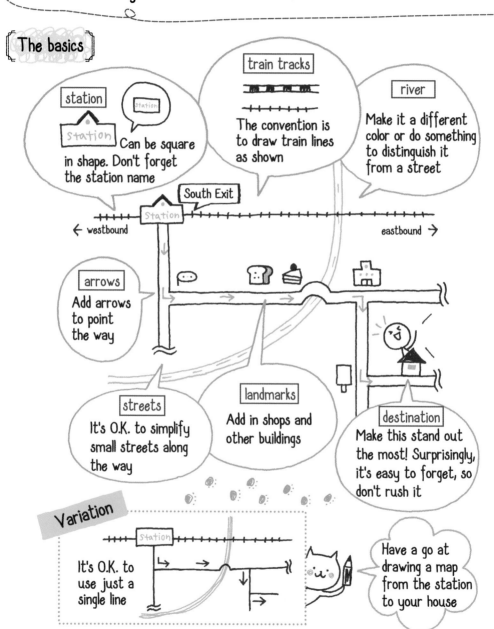

station

Can be square in shape. Don't forget the station name

train tracks

The convention is to draw train lines as shown

river

Make it a different color or do something to distinguish it from a street

South Exit

← westbound

eastbound →

arrows

Add arrows to point the way

streets

It's O.K. to simplify small streets along the way

landmarks

Add in shops and other buildings

destination

Make this stand out the most! Surprisingly, it's easy to forget, so don't rush it

Variation

It's O.K. to use just a single line

Have a go at drawing a map from the station to your house

Buildings

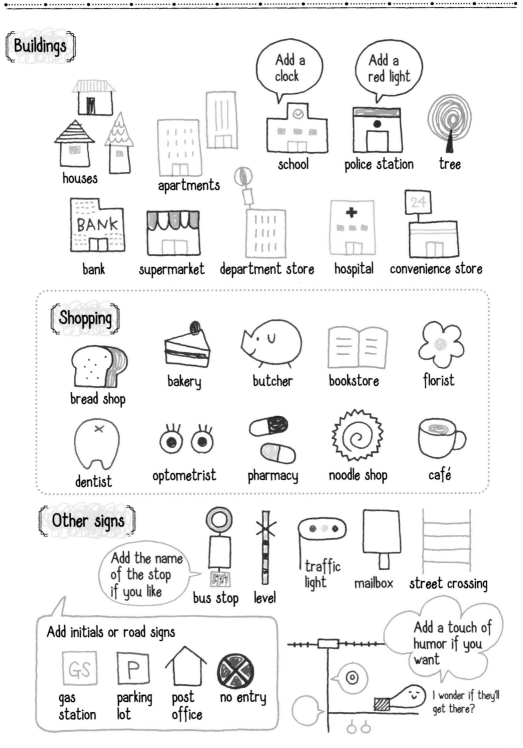

Add a clock

Add a red light

houses

apartments

school

police station

tree

bank

supermarket

department store

hospital

convenience store

Shopping

bread shop

bakery

butcher

bookstore

florist

dentist

optometrist

pharmacy

noodle shop

café

Other signs

Add the name of the stop if you like

bus stop

level

traffic light

mailbox

street crossing

Add initials or road signs

gas station

parking lot

post office

no entry

Add a touch of humor if you want

I wonder if they'll get there?

Illustrations from various countries to use in a travel journal

Illustrations that depict foreign countries are great for using in travel journals and scrapbooks. If the people are too tough, just draw the landmarks and iconic images associated with that country.

France

The famous Eiffel Tower looks stylish depicted in a line drawing

England

Red double-decker buses are quintessentially English

Switzerland

Draw the Alps and an alpenhorn

Germany

The houses are like fairy tale cottages

USA

A log house hits the right note

Hawaii

A hibiscus has five petals

China

Bring out the feel of each country using mountains and clouds

India

Simplify World Heritage sites in line drawings

Korea

Don't forget the bold upward curve of the roof

Japan

3,000 feet

2,000 feet

36

Focus on defining characteristics to simplify fairy tale drawings

Fairy tale characters and settings are a great subject to explore. If it's too difficult to make them look authentic, focus on the characteristics of each story to create simple pictures.

Red Riding Hood

Make Red Riding Hood a bit chubby and draw her with her hood on

Base the wolf on a dog, but make the ears pointy and add fangs

The woodsman

Other characters

Grandmother

Cinderella

Draw an adult woman with a tall, slender physique

Momotaro, or Peach Boy

Rounded mountains make for a "once upon a time" look

Bangs and a topknot define Momotaro. Add a monkey, dog and pheasant to complete his retinue

Legend of Lady Kaguya

Japanese-style clouds

Draw black hair parted in the center. Don't worry about drawing all the layers of her ceremonial robes

1,001 Nights

If the story's setting is aptly captured, just a few different colors and simple lines are needed

107

Tracing Time

Place thin paper over the top of the illustrations featured
so far and trace them as many times as you like.

Disappointed

LET'S DOODLE!

well done

LESSON 4
Lively Decorations for Cards and Parties

Try using illustrations to decorate cards and notes. You can also add illustrations to invitations and party favors.

Cards

Add illustrations to seasonal greeting cards, party invitations and other gift cards—an already heartfelt gesture is made even more so. Drawing from the heart is sure to convey your feelings to the recipient.

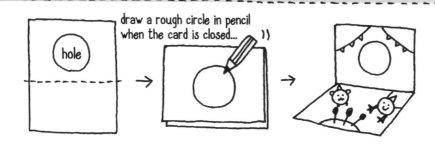

draw a rough circle in pencil when the card is closed...

hole

Glass and Plastic

Personalize and embellish glass and plastic items.
Just be sure to take your time and be precise.
You can't erase and start over!

Pens that can draw on glass and plastic

Draw slowly as if applying ink

⚠ Before drawing, wipe off any oil or dirt as they will repel the ink

Menus

A hand-decorated
menu really stands
out and makes a
regular meal into
a special event. Customize the menu to
reflect the type of food being served.

Draw on dark
colored paper

Ink flows more
smoothly than with
normal ballpoint pens

It takes a little while for
the ink to take on shape and
definition, so just wait for it
to develop without disturbing it

Party Items

Personalize party cups
by drawing guests' faces
and adding their names.
Decorations around the
edges of paper plates add an
unexpectedly festive touch.
Hang flags around the room to
make the mood even livelier.

Template

Fold paper over and
cut to the size of
the paper template

Draw on
the flags

Pass a string along the
fold line and glue together

のり

Create an adorable row of repeated decorative motifs

Decorative motifs can be used around the edges of illustrations, messages and so on. Repeating the same motif at regular intervals is the secret to getting a cute result.

[Basic repetitions]

There are all sorts of motifs. Match the type of repetition to the motif

(A)

(A + a)

(A + A' + A")

(A + B + A' + B')

(A + B + C + B + A)

(A + B + C + D + E)

• •• etc.

Various repeating patterns

Borders galore

All kinds of corners

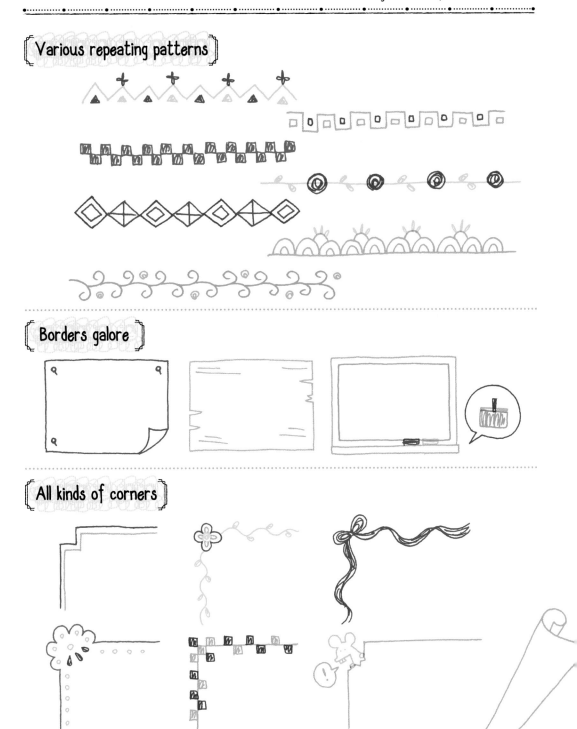

38 Stick to the rules when creating decorative fonts

Letters and characters, whether English, Japanese, Chinese or otherwise, really come to life when you have something important to say.

Rules for decorative fonts

Decide on how to unify the font, such as making all letters the same size

Make vertical strokes slightly bigger

Make vertical strokes broader

Add a dot at the start and finish of each stroke

Add a curl to each curved section

It's the same for Chinese characters

Large vertical strokes

Color in blank spaces

Round out corners

・・・ Etc.

one step

There are rules for the fonts used in publishing, too

〈MS Mincho〉

Horizontal is narrow

Vertical is thick

〈 Gothic 〉

All the same thickness

Decorations using words

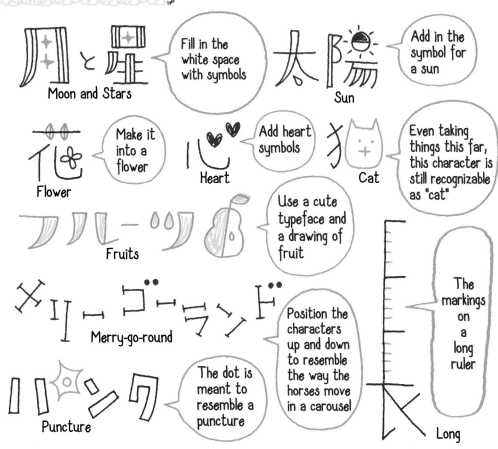

Moon and Stars

Fill in the white space with symbols

Sun

Add in the symbol for a sun

Flower

Make it into a flower

Heart

Add heart symbols

Cat

Even taking things this far, this character is still recognizable as "cat"

Fruits

Use a cute typeface and a drawing of fruit

Merry-go-round

Position the characters up and down to resemble the way the horses move in a carousel

Puncture

The dot is meant to resemble a puncture

Long

The markings on a long ruler

Alphabet

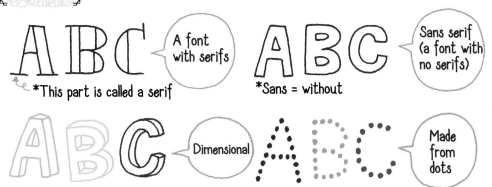

A font with serifs

*This part is called a serif

Sans serif (a font with no serifs)

*Sans = without

Dimensional

Made from dots

117

39 Frame congratulatory messages in color

Cards with congratulatory messages or joyful announcements need to convey the happiness of the occasion, so make them colorful.

[Birthdays]

Name

HAPPY BIRTHDAY

Happy birthday!

Asian-style

[Weddings]

Dear Louise,

Congratulations on your marriage

I feel like the mother of the bride

Wedding Bells

George & Louise

TIP

Adding items or seasonal objects that the recipient likes is sure to be a hit

She likes cats, so...

It's June, so...

Baby shower

Congratulations on your new baby

〈Stork〉

the tips of the wings and tail are black

red legs

Moving day

Come to visit

We've moved!

Keep it simple with a truck

Address

Nearest train station

Special occasions

These can be used for celebrating various events such as passing an exam, winning an award or starting a new job

(Pass) You did it!

Bravo!

Congrats!

on your job offer!

Good job!

119

40 Add seasonal touches to frames and gifts

Capture the spirit of the season with decorative doodles, adding the colors and images associated with the holiday or time of year.

Christmas

merry X'mas

I hope Santa visits you!

Merry Christmas!

Merry Christmas

Stick to simple outlines and shapes

Draw the face of the recipient if you like

New Year's Day

How big is your baby now?

HAPPY NEW YEAR

Add a short message

Items that make good frames

Winter

Let it snow!

Make the bottom section big so that the message fits in easily

Warm Winter Wishes

Summertime

Don't forget the sunblock!

August x

Add the date if you wish

❀ Summer: from the end of the rainy season until the start of fall

❀ Late summer: from mid-August to the start of fall

It's so hot every day!

Keep your cool!

In hot weather, draw something hot!

A drawing that evokes a feeling of coolness ←

Conversely, a drawing that evokes feeling hot →

41 Brief messages can be written anywhere

You can write little messages and memos anywhere. Keep practicing to create your own style.

Little messages

Thank you so much! I had a great time!

With thanks

Thank you

Thanks for dinner!

Include motifs with thank you notes

thank you

THANKS

ヨロシク!
Thanks in advance!

Announcement

Please!

おつかれさま =3
Thanks for your hard work

Or try it in a foreign language

ごめんなさい
Sorry

Good luck!

Sorry

Change the expression to suit various uses

Secret

Add doodles to notes and lists

POINT

Use a miniature light bulb to highlight a key point

IMPORTANT

An arrow points to something important

テストに出る
Will be on the test

CHECK ✓

Check the box

Well done　Average　OK　Disappointed　Fail!　I'll do my best　Satisfied

ex. (for example)　etc. (etcetera)　cf. (refer to)

Teachers' faces

Frames and notes

Don't forget!

To buy today:
• stamps
• fall cardigan
• warm socks

SALE

Event details

Carnivores welcome

There'll be veggies at the BBQ too

BBQ information
• Date and time:
• Place: _____
※ Please bring something to share

123

42

Keep time, place and occasion in mind when creating office messages

Personal messages to colleagues or coworkers tell them of important developments in the office or alert them to upcoming events.

For everyday use

To your boss or seniors

To your coworkers or juniors

Return the call!

To B

To A   from Z

☑ You had a call
☐ They will call again
☑ Please call them

0000 - 0000

Message   It's regarding the quotation

Time: 11:20   Taken by Ⓚ

The boss called your internal line at 3 pm

Good luck! Ⓚ

An old-style phone looks cute

Bye, I'm finished for the day

Make sure the message gets through and isn't too playful in tone

Add a few illustrations to boost motivation

Use an analog clock set to the appointment time to add appeal

To do today!

9:00 ✉ send mail
10:00   look for documents
2:00   meeting
approx. 3:00

· corrections
· ask for quote
· 3 comprehensive package plans

Must do: Go home on the train!

P15

Leave at 1:30 for meeting with Y

Returning at 4

For parties

I love beer!

I'll have a couple of cocktails

gotcha!

Tonight's party
8 PM
See you there!

Welcome party
for new staff
Darius **and** Edie

○ Month   × Year   6:30
(Price: $10 each)

office | here
Bar xxx |

Please be punctual

Staff
party

Time:
Venue

For various occasions

♥ Frank

Collection for
xx the newlywed

☐ A   ☐ B
☐ D   ☐ E
☐ G   ☑
※ I'll buy a gift voucher for him

Thank
you
Cora

For poor
Gus

ouch!

Let's cheer
him up!

Make advertising stand out

43 Illustrations work well on price tags or any form of advertising. Make your items stand out in your store, shop or online business, and watch your profits soar.

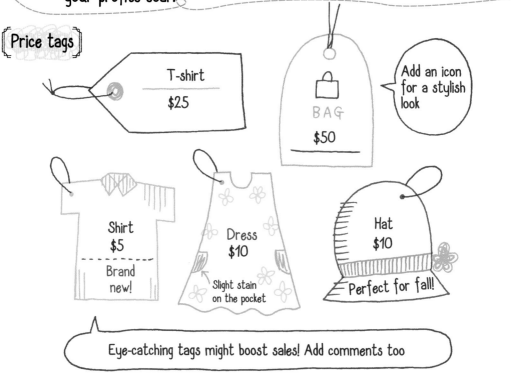

Food

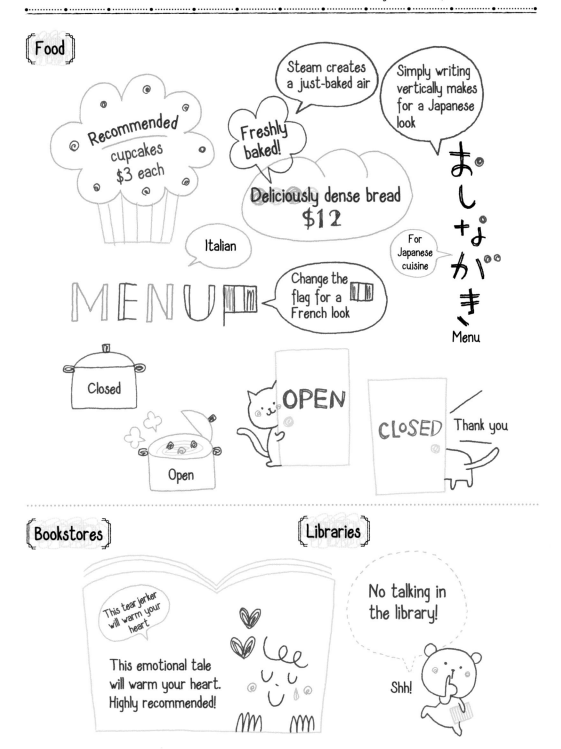

Steam creates a just-baked air

Simply writing vertically makes for a Japanese look

Recommended cupcakes $3 each

Freshly baked!

Deliciously dense bread $12

おしながき
Menu

Italian

For Japanese cuisine

Change the flag for a French look

MENU

Closed

Open

OPEN

CLOSED

Thank you

Bookstores

This tear jerker will warm your heart

This emotional tale will warm your heart. Highly recommended!

Libraries

No talking in the library!

Shh!

Published by Tuttle Publishing, an imprint of Periplus Editions (HK) Ltd

www.tuttlepublishing.com

BALL PEN DE KANTAN! PETIT KAWAII ILLUST GA KAKERU HON
Copyright © Studio Dunk, Kamo 2011
All rights reserved
English translation rights arranged with Mates Publishing Co., Ltd
Through Japan UNI Agency, Inc., Tokyo

ISBN 978-4-8053-1585-9

English Translation ©2019 Periplus Editions (HK) Ltd.

Distributed by

North America, Latin America &
Europe
Tuttle Publishing
364 Innovation Drive
North Clarendon, VT 05759-9436
U.S.A.
Tel: 1 (802) 773-8930
Fax: 1 (802) 773-6993
info@tuttlepublishing.com
www.tuttlepublishing.com

Japan
Tuttle Publishing
Yaekari Building 3rd Floor
5-4-12 Osaki
Shinagawa-ku
Tokyo 141-0032
Tel: (81) 3 5437-0171
Fax: (81) 3 5437-0755
sales@tuttle.co.jp
www.tuttle.co.jp

Asia Pacific
Berkeley Books Pte. Ltd.
3 Kallang Sector #04-01
Singapore 349278
Tel: (65) 67412178
Fax: (65) 67412179
inquiries@periplus.com.sg
www.tuttlepublishing.com

Printed in Malaysia   2112VP

25 24 23 22   11 10 9 8 7 6

TUTTLE PUBLISHING® is a registered trademark of Tuttle Publishing, a division of Periplus Editions (HK) Ltd.

"Books to Span the East and West"

Tuttle Publishing was founded in 1832 in the small New England town of Rutland, Vermont [USA]. Our core values remain as strong today as they were then—to publish best-in-class books which bring people together one page at a time. In 1948, we established a publishing office in Japan—and Tuttle is now a leader in publishing English-language books about the arts, languages and cultures of Asia. The world has become a much smaller place today and Asia's economic and cultural influence has grown. Yet the need for meaningful dialogue and information about this diverse region has never been greater. Over the past seven decades, Tuttle has published thousands of books on subjects ranging from martial arts and paper crafts to language learning and literature—and our talented authors, illustrators, designers and photographers have won many prestigious awards. We welcome you to explore the wealth of information available on Asia at www.tuttlepublishing.com.